Trust in Modern Societies

Jean Stockard
Winter, 1998

To my children
Berenika and Blaise